CW00539297

The Lads from Liverpool

Chris Banks

M20

The Lads from Liverpool

The railway photography of John Corkill and Peter Hanson

Compiled by Chris Banks

In memory of
Carol Ann Corkill
1945-2013

SLP
Silver Link Publishing Ltd

First published in 2015

British Library Cataloguing in Publication Data

A catalogue record for this book is available from the British Library.

ISBN 978 1 85794 443 3

Silver Link Publishing Ltd
The Trundle
Ringstead Road
Great Addington
Kettering
Northants NN14 4BW

Tel/Fax: 01536 330588
email: sales@nostalgiacollection.com
Website: www.nostalgiacollection.com

Printed and bound in the Czech Republic

Contents

Frontispiece: Stanier 5MT 4-6-0 No. 45312 arrives at Liverpool Exchange Station with another 'Black Five' No. 45219 waiting to leave in June 1963, with No. 2 signalbox in the background. No. 45312 has a painted Wigan Spring's Branch 8F shed code on itssmokebox door. This was during its short stay at Wigan, from 22 June to 6 July when it transferred to Edge Hill. No. 45219 was based at Bradford Low Moor. *John Corkill.*

Title spread left: 'King' Class 4-6-0 No 6017 *King Edward IV* gently starts away from a deserted London Paddington station with an express for Wolverhampton on Tuesday 8 August 1961. On 2 July 1928 No 6017 was allocated new to Old Oak Common shed after being constructed at Swindon Works, and during its working life it was also based at Bristol Bath Road and Plymouth Laira. It also spent time at Wolverhampton Stafford Road from 20 September 1928 to 5 November 1939, and 2 February 1959 until withdrawal on 23 July 1962, having completed 1,853,262 miles in service. *John Corkill*

Introduction

John Corkill and Peter Hanson were both working railwaymen during the closing years of steam traction, working in the Liverpool area and still living there today. John started work in August 1957 at Edge Hill shed as an apprentice fitter, moving to Sutton Oak depot at St Helens from January to April 1963 before returning to Edge Hill, where he worked with steam locomotives through to the closure of the shed in May 1968. Peter started work for British Railways in September 1953 at the former Cheshire Lines Committee (CLC) Brunswick goods depot delivery office, and after National Service returned to the railway at Birkenhead Morpeth Docks goods offices. Further moves saw him working at the freight accounts section at Liverpool Waterloo Dock, which had to move to different premises near Lime Street station in 1967 after a disastrous fire.

Throughout this period both John and Peter photographed the disappearing steam locomotives and the changing railway scene, providing a remarkable and unique record of this unforgettable time in the history of British Railways. The North West, and the Liverpool area in particular, is extensively covered, with a special focus on Edge Hill engine shed.

A previous volume of photographs by John and Peter was published in the Silver Link 'Classic Steam' series in 1995, and this new publication is a second volume containing more than 170 further images, all previously unpublished. Today both John and Peter are retired and have between them a rich source of memories from their railway careers, as well as capturing a past way of life in these nostalgic views, now more than 50 years ago. These scenes from the past encapsulate the real essence of the end of the steam era and provide a fascinating glimpse of a bygone age from the cameras of these 'Lads from Liverpool'.

Title spread right: The Hawksworth-designed 'County' Class 4-6-0s were the ultimate locomotives in the development of two-cylinder 4-6-0 express engines on the GWR, and were distinguished from the company's other 4-6-0 designs in having one long splasher covering all the driving wheels, and a straight nameplate. The first of the class entered traffic on 4 August 1945 and was fitted with a double blastpipe and chimney, separately cast cylinders, and a hopper ashpan to make servicing easier. Thirty were built, the last, No 1029 entering traffic on 10 April 1947. At first the engines did not carry nameplates, but from No 1017 onwards this was changed, and names were applied. The first member of the class, No 1000, had to wait until March 1946 before being named *County of Middlesex*. This view shows No 1022 *County of Northampton* light engine at Oxford in 1957, with the locomotive shed in the background; at the time it was allocated to Chester GWR shed. It had entered traffic on 24 December 1946, allocated to Plymouth Laira. It stayed in the West Country until December 1951 when Shrewsbury added it to its allocation, then on to Chester after a few weeks. It returned to Shrewsbury in June 1958 and, after a short spell at Hereford in 1959, remained at Shrewsbury until withdrawn on 5 October 1962. *Peter Hanson*

1024

Western Region

Left: One of the Chester-based 'County' Class 4-6-0s, No 1024 *County of Pembroke*, takes water at Shrewsbury station in August 1957 while working a northbound express. Dating from January 1947, the locomotive spent its first years based at Wolverhampton Stafford Road before moving to Plymouth Laira in February 1951, then on to Old Oak Common in October 1952. After a month it moved to Chester, with later transfers to Bristol Bath Road as well as St Philip's Marsh and finally Swindon, from where withdrawal came on 8 April 1964, with a mileage of 643,975. *Peter Hanson*

Right: 'Castle' Class 4-6-0 No 5019 *Treago Castle* nears the top of Hollinwood Bank, between Wem and Whitchurch in Shropshire, with the 2.10pm Paddington to Birkenhead express in May 1962, when allocated to Wolverhampton Stafford Road. Built in January 1932, the 'Castle' had spent most of its time based in the West County and came to Stafford Road from Bristol Bath Road on 8 May 1958. It was withdrawn on 21 September 1962. *Peter Hanson*

Left: One of the first batch of 'Castle' Class 4-6-0s to be built, No 4081 *Warwick Castle* storms out of Shrewsbury with an express for Bristol in January 1959. The 'Castle' entered traffic at Old Oak Common in April 1924, and when this scene was recorded was allocated to Bristol Bath Road. The final allocation was Carmarthen, where withdrawal came on 1 January 1963. *Peter Hanson*

Right: On 27 July 1959 is this view at St Erth station with 'Castle' Class 4-6-0 No 5035 *Coity Castle* working the London-bound 'Cornish Riviera Express' formed of coaching stock in 'chocolate and cream' livery. No 5035 went new to Cardiff Canton in May 1935 and moved to Wolverhampton Stafford Road seven months later. On 20 April 1940 it was transferred to Old Oak Common, where it stayed until the final move to Swindon on 6 September 1960, from where withdrawal came on 17 May 1962. *Peter Hanson*

PLATFORM
1
5035
PLATFORM
2

Above: Another 'Castle' Class 4-6-0, No 5021 *Whittington Castle*, is in charge of the 'City of Plymouth Holiday Express' at Truro station also on Monday 27 July 1959. This was during the time that the engine was based at Plymouth Laira, and is seen here coupled to a Hawksworth flat-sided tender. Its final allocation was Cardiff Canton, from where withdrawal came on 21 September 1962, after 30 years of service. *Peter Hanson*

Right: '2800' Class 2-8-0 No 2809 passes Totnes with an evening freight working to Plymouth on Wednesday 29 July 1959, with '5101' Class 2-6-2T No 4108 in the background, outside the goods shed. The '2800' Class was a Churchward design and the GWR's first 2-8-0 type. No 2809 came into service in October 1905 and retained its rather spartan cab; later examples, built from 1938, had side window cabs, affording better protection for the crew. No 2809 had been allocated to Plymouth Laira since September 1958 and remained there until withdrawn in January 1960. *Peter Hanson*

Opposite: Freight traffic at Bristol St Philip's Marsh, with 'Grange' Class 4-6-0 No 6833 *Calcot Grange*, allocated to the nearby shed, passing by. These were a Collett design that was a version of the 'Hall' Class, but with smaller wheels. No 6833 dated from August 1937 and was first allocated to Wolverhampton Oxley. After serving from a number of sheds, including Tyseley (Birmingham) and Leamington Spa, it returned to Oxley in May 1962 where withdrawal came on 10 October 1965. *John Corkill*

M421124

S·L·S
SPECIAL
7802

Left: At Shrewsbury station on a wet Sunday 17 January 1965, 'Manor' Class 4-6-0 No 7802 *Bradley Manor*, bearing its 6F Machynlleth shed plate, has been specially prepared for an SLS special. This tour was to have been the last train on the Ruabon to Barmouth line, as well as the Welshpool to Whitchurch route, but due to flood damage earlier in the month the Ruabon-Barmouth portion of the tour had to be cancelled. Instead, the route taken was from Shrewsbury to Welshpool, Oswestry, Whitchurch, and back to Oswestry and Shrewsbury. In addition, the tour made a 'last train' run over the Llanfyllin branch, hauled by a '63xx' 2-6-0, No 7802 taking over again at Gobowen for the return to Shrewsbury. No 7802 was added to stock on 22 January 1938 and saw service at sheds including Bristol Bath Road and St Philip's Marsh, Oswestry and Tyseley. Shortly after this tour it was transferred to Shrewsbury, where withdrawal came on 6 November 1965. Sold to Woodham's scrapyard at Barry, it was rescued in 1979 and later restored. *John Corkill*

Above: In filthy condition, 'Manor' Class 4-6-0 No 7824 *Iford Manor* approaches Welshpool with the London-bound 'Cambrian Coast Express' in July 1964. The engine was allocated to Oxley, Wolverhampton, at the time, which perhaps gives a clue to its uncleaned state, as Cambrian-based 'Manors' were noted for their well-turned-out appearance. No 7824 entered service under British Railways on 12 December 1950 and was first allocated to Cheltenham Malvern Road, a sub-shed to Gloucester Horton Road. It finished its days at Oxley, withdrawal coming in November 1964. *Peter Hanson*

The platforms at Dovey Junction reflect a very wet August day in 1957, with Machynlleth-allocated '2251' Class 0-6-0 No 2255 awaiting departure on the 1.35pm service to Pwllheli. The class was designed by Collett for mixed-traffic work as replacements for the much older 'Dean Goods' type. They were popular with enginemen as they had comfortable large cabs with side windows, and were lively runners. No 2255 dated from March 1930 and spent its BR days working on the Cambrian lines until withdrawn in May 1962. *Peter Hanson*

Western Region

'4900' 'Hall' Class 4-6-0 No 6958 *Oxburgh Hall* was a visitor to Crewe South shed on Sunday 30 October 1960, while allocated to Pontypool Road shed. A Collett design, two batches were built between 1928 and 1931, and 1940 and 1943. No 6958 was the last to be built in April 1943, followed in March 1944 by the 'Modified Halls', a Hawksworth design with welded plate frames and individually cast cylinders. No 6958 later moved to Cardiff East Dock and finally Worcester before being withdrawn in June 1965. Behind the locomotive is the Crewe South coaling plant, erected by the LNWR in 1920 at a cost of £10,000, and modified by the LMS in the 1930s, which included the installation of a steel-framed wagon hoist. *John Corkill*

Wellington shed in Shropshire provides storage space for 'Modified Hall' Class 4-6-0 No 7922 *Salford Hall* with sacking over the chimney to keep the rain out, but with a fully coaled tender. Wellington was a small shed with an allocation of only around 16 engines, which were all tank designs, so the presence of No 7922 was somewhat unusual. The date is Sunday 18 January 1959, when No 7922 was allocated to Shrewsbury. Entering traffic in September 1950, it was sent new to Chester GWR shed, then, after allocation to a number of other depots, including Tyseley, Stourbridge and Southall, it finally settled at Oxford, where withdrawal came in December 1965. *Peter Hanson*

Above: On Sunday 30 August 1959 Oswestry shed is home to 'Manor' Class 4-6-0 No 7801 *Anthony Manor* – the tender is filled with some extremely large lumps of coal for the fireman to cope with. This engine entered service on 21 January 1938 at Bristol Bath Road shed and moved to St Philip's Marsh at the end of November 1939, where it stayed until May 1948 when its new home became Plymouth Laira. It moved north to Chester in October 1953 and to Oswestry on 26 August 1958. Final transfer was to Shrewsbury in December 1962 and withdrawal in July 1965. *Peter Hanson*

Below: Also to be seen at Oswestry shed on the same day was '7400' Class 0-6-0PT No 7410. This was a Collett design similar to the '6400' Class, but without the equipment for working push-pull trains. No 7410 dated from December 1936 and spent its British Railways days at Oswestry, apart from three months at Machynlleth in 1954, and was withdrawn in January 1961. Note the metal-framed carriage and van in the background, without their wheels, in use as storage sheds. *Peter Hanson*

Left: Peter visited Penzance shed on Monday 27 July 1959 to find the shed's own 'County' Class 4-6-0 No 1006 *County of Cornwall* awaiting work. Allocated new to Plymouth Laira on 29 December 1945, it spent most of its working life based at West Country sheds, apart from a four-month stay at Carmarthen in 1954. Little work could be found for steam traction when diesel power took over many of the workings, so on 15 December 1962 the 'County' was transferred to Swindon shed and withdrawn on 17 September of the following year. *Peter Hanson*

Right: 'Castle' Class 4-6-0 No 4081 *Warwick Castle* was seen earlier in action leaving Shrewsbury, and in this view, on a Sunday in February 1959, it is ready to leave Shrewsbury shed to take up its rostered duty. Withdrawal came from Carmarthen on 1 January 1963 *Peter Hanson*

We stay in the West Country to visit Plymouth Laira shed on Tuesday 28 July to view 'Castle' Class 4-6-0 No 5089 *Westminster Abbey*, allocated to Wolverhampton Stafford Road at the time. Added to stock in November 1939, it spent its first nine years operating from Swansea Landore shed before moving to Cardiff Canton. It spent time allocated to Plymouth Laira from April 1956 to May 1958, then went to Wolverhampton. When Stafford Road shed closed in September 1963, No 5089 moved into the care of Oxley shed, until withdrawal in November 1964. *Peter Hanson*

Also on shed on that day, standing alongside the Plymouth Laira coaling stage and having its smokebox cleaned, is Old Oak Common-based 'King' Class 4-6-0 No 6003 *King George IV*. Entering service in July 1927, it was based at Old Oak Common until 13 September 1960, when it transferred to Cardiff Canton, returning to Old Oak on 15 February 1962, where withdrawal came on 25 June after a few months in store. *Peter Hanson*

'Merchant Navy' Class 4-6-2 No 35028 *Clan Line* awaits departure from London Waterloo for Southampton on Monday 12 June 1967, in excellent external condition. The 'Pacific' entered traffic on 23 December 1948 and was first allocated to Bournemouth. It moved to Dover during October 1949, Stewarts Lane in March 1950, and to Nine Elms in June 1959. Weymouth added it to its allocation in August 1964, then it returned to Nine Elms in April 1967. Naming did not take place until 15 January 1951, when the ceremony was carried out at Southampton Docks by Lord Rotherwick, Chairman of the Clan Line shipping company. The locomotive was rebuilt at Eastleigh Works, with its 'air-smoothed' casing removed, in September 1959. As can be seen, the nameplates were removed during the last months of the engine's operating life, with withdrawal coming on 9 July 1967, the last day of steam operation on the Southern Region, when all the remaining steam sheds closed at midnight. On Sunday 2 July No 35028 worked one of the two Southern official 'Farewell to Steam' specials from Waterloo to Bournemouth, and had its nameplates restored for the occasion. Following withdrawal, after clocking up 794,391 miles, No 35028 was purchased by the Merchant Navy Preservation Society. *John Corkill*

Rebuilt 'Merchant Navy' Class 4-6-2 No 35008 *Orient Line* enters London Waterloo from Bournemouth on Wednesday 7 September 1966, with the flats of the period in the background. This was the locomotive that worked the second of the official 'Farewell to Steam' specials on 2 July 1967, taking 11 coaches to Weymouth. The relatively poor response to these excursions was no doubt due to the high fares and lack of publicity. Five trains were originally planned, but the two that did run proved more than ample for the number of passengers. No 35008 was withdrawn from Nine Elms on 9 July 1967 and, after a number of months in storage at the shed, was sold for scrap. *John Corkill*

Rebuilt 'West Country' Class 4-6-2 No 34032 *Camelford* leaves Bournemouth with a passenger working from Weymouth to Waterloo on Friday 9 September 1966. New to traffic on 18 June 1946, its first allocation was Ramsgate shed. It was then based at a number of depots, including Stewarts Lane, Exmouth Junction and Plymouth Friary. The final allocation was Salisbury, from 11 November 1963 until withdrawal on 2 October 1966, after which it was sold for scrap. *John Corkill*

'Merchant Navy' Class 4-6-2 No 35012 *United States Lines* leaves Eastleigh on Wednesday 7 September 1966 with the down 'Bournemouth Belle'. Built at Eastleigh Works and entering traffic on 13 January 1945, No 35012 was rebuilt in February 1957. It received its nameplates on 10 April 1945, the naming being carried out by Admiral Schuirman of the United States Navy at a ceremony at Waterloo station. The engine's first allocation was to London's Nine Elms shed, and during its active service it operated from Bournemouth and Weymouth, returning to Nine Elms by 17 April 1967, with withdrawal a few days later. One interesting duty it performed was on Friday 24 April 1964, when it towed 'A4' 4-6-2 No 60008 *Dwight D. Eisenhower* to Southampton for shipment to the American Railroad Museum at Green Bay. The locomotive was turned out in gleaming condition, and the Museum's President was so impressed with No 35012 that, on its withdrawal, he said he would also welcome it as another resident of the Museum. However, this was not to be, for after storage at Nine Elms and Weymouth *United States Lines* was eventually cut up. *John Corkill*

The following day, 8 September 1966, sees 'Standard' 4MT 2-6-4T No 80140, allocated to Feltham, taking a mixed freight through Eastleigh. Built at Brighton Works, it was first allocated to Neasden shed, London, on 10 June 1956, which was then part of the Eastern Region. When the regional boundaries changed on 23 February 1958 Neasden became part of the London Midland Region, and a decision was made to transfer all the Southern Region's Fairburn 4MT 2-6-4Ts to the LMR, and an equal number of 'Standard' 2-6-4Ts from the LMR in exchange. In December 1959 all ten 'Standards' at Neasden left for the Southern, including No 80140, which went to Tunbridge Wells West. It later operated from Brighton and Redhill, before going to Feltham in May 1965. In October 1966 it finally went to Nine Elms, withdrawal coming on 9 July 1967. No 80140 was later sold for scrap. *John Corkill*

Left: In poor external condition, BR Standard 4MT 4-6-0 No 75074 waits to leave Portsmouth Harbour station with a local passenger train to Eastleigh on Wednesday 7 September 1966. Built at Swindon Works, it is seen here with a double chimney, fitted in July 1961, and paired with a BRIB 4,725-gallon tender. On 18 November 1955 its first allocation was to Exmouth Junction, followed by a series of moves to Eastleigh, Basingstoke, Stewarts Lane and Norwood Junction. A return to Eastleigh in May 1965 was its last move, and it remained in service until 9 July 1967. By the end of that month it was at Salisbury shed, together with another 53 stored steam locomotives awaiting scrapping. *John Corkill*

Bottom left: Awaiting departure at Farnborough station on the same day is 'Battle of Britain' Class 4-6-2 No 34071, formerly *601 Squadron* – part of the nameplate is still in situ. This was an Eastleigh-based engine, going there from Nine Elms in September 1964. It was withdrawn on 30 April 1967, after amassing a mileage of 782,028 since entering traffic at Dover shed on 17 April 1948. *John Corkill*

Right: 'West Country' Class 4-6-2 No 34013 *Okehampton* entered traffic on 30 October 1945 at Exmouth Junction and was rebuilt in September 1957, while in Eastleigh Works for a general overhaul. On re-entering traffic the 'Pacific' was reallocated to Bricklayers Arms shed, then to Brighton on 2 July 1962, and finally Salisbury in September 1963. Salisbury had an enviable reputation for a high standard of maintenance and for turning out its engines in excellent condition, as can be seen in this view of No 34013 at Southampton, also on 7 September 1966. This was another locomotive that kept going until 9 July 1967, but after storage it was scrapped. *John Corkill*

OKEHAMPTON
7P5FA
34013

Above: What a contrast in condition to No 34013! This is the same location at Southampton on the following day, Thursday 8 September 1966, and no credit to its Eastleigh home is 'Battle of Britain' 4-6-2 No 34077 603 *Squadron*, profusely leaking steam from between the frames and elsewhere as it awaits departure for London Waterloo. Withdrawal came on 26 March 1967. *John Corkill*

On Sunday 18 June 1967 the RCTS arranged a 'Farewell to Southern Steam' tour from Waterloo to Weymouth, which included a visit to Weymouth shed and a run down the branch line to Swanage. This was to be the last privately sponsored steam-hauled train on the Southern with, at the time, no further prospects of steam ever running again there after 9 July. The tour was run in conjunction with the Southern Railwaymen's Home for Children at Woking, which benefited from the tour's profit of £1,400. Leaving London, the train was double-headed by BR Standard 5MT 4-6-0 No 73029 and unrebuilt 'West Country' Class 4-6-2 No 34023 *Blackmore Vale*. At Fareham the two locomotives were replaced by rebuilt 'Battle of Britain' Class 4-6-2 No 34089 602 *Squadron*, and at Southampton rebuilt 'West Country' Class 4-6-2 No 34108 *Wincanton* was attached as pilot. On arrival at Wareham, No 34108 left to proceed light engine to Weymouth, while No 34089 worked the train down the Swanage branch with 'Standard' 4MT 2-6-4T No 80146 attached at the rear. On returning to Wareham, No 34089 hauled the train unaided to Weymouth, with a stop at Radipole Halt for those wishing to visit the shed. The return working was double-headed by Nos 34023 and 34108 through to Salisbury, where they were replaced by 'Merchant Navy' Class 4-6-2 No 35013 *Blue Funnel* for the rest of the run back to London. Participants were issued with an itinerary that finished with the words: 'Southern steam, you will not be forgotten. May your successors serve in the future as faithfully as you did in the past.'

Right: Here the RCTS special awaits departure from Swanage behind No 80146. Built at Brighton Works, the 2-6-4T went new to Brighton shed on 30 October 1956. Withdrawal came on 9 July 1967, from Bournemouth shed, and the engine was later sold for scrap. *John Corkill*

RCTS
80146
SPL
12
SPL
12

This is Weymouth shed, with the three 'Pacifics' gathered to be serviced after working in on the RCTS special; all were now shorn of their nameplates. No 34023 was one of the last unrebuilt examples in service, and had entered traffic at Ramsgate shed on 4 February 1946. Withdrawal came on 9 July 1967, but the 'West Country' was later purchased for preservation. *John Corkill*

Rebuilt 'Battle of Britain' Class 4-6-2 No 34089 602 *Squadron*, its duties done for the day, rests on Weymouth shed. The coaling stage in the background is pure Great Western in design, as Weymouth shed was originally GWR and opened in 1885. The ramped coaling stage was built in 1930, replacing an earlier smaller structure. The LSWR also had a shed at Weymouth, which was a small two-road structure situated alongside the station. In the 1930s the station was extended and the lines rearranged, resulting in the shed having to be demolished. It closed in January 1939, after an agreement had been reached with the GWR for joint use of the latter's shed. Coded 82F under the Western Region, it became part of the Southern Region in February 1958 and was recoded 71G, which changed to 70G in September 1963. Closure came on 9 July 1967. No 34089 was withdrawn on the same day, from Salisbury shed. *John Corkill*

Rebuilt 'West Country' Class 4-6-2 No 34108 *Wincanton* takes water ready for the return run of the RCTS special as far as Salisbury. New to Bournemouth shed in April 1950, it was rebuilt as late as March 1961. Withdrawal from Salisbury shed came seven days after this visit to Weymouth. *John Corkill*

We now cross the Solent to the Isle of Wight on Saturday 21 August 1965, and at Ryde Esplanade station find 'O2' Class 0-4-4T No 31 *Chale* waiting to run along the Pier to collect its train. Built at Nine Elms Works in April 1890, this Adams-designed engine was withdrawn on 19 March 1967 together with No 24 *Calbourne*; they were the last 'O2' engines in service and their passing marked the end of steam on the Island. *John Corkill*

Above: A little later 'O2' *Chale* runs down the Pier with its train for Ventnor – the end of Pier Head station can be seen in the background. The Ventnor to Shanklin part of the route closed on 18 April 1966. *John Corkill*

Right: The following day, Sunday 22 August 1965, was thoroughly wet as 'O2' Class 0-4-4T No 22 *Brading* waits at Ryde Esplanade to run along the Pier. This 'O2' succumbed to withdrawal on 1 January 1967, together with another seven class members. *John Corkill*

No 22 *Brading* has returned from Pier Head station and waits to leave Ryde Esplanade with its train for Shanklin. The line to Shanklin is now the only route open, operated today by former London Transport tube stock dating from 1938. There are six two-car units on the island, with two required for the daily services. *John Corkill*

5
21
11
SOUTHERN R
PASSEN
MUST NOT
THE LINE

Left: 'O2' Class 0-4-4T No 21 *Sandown* waits for the signal to leave Ryde Esplanade to go to Ryde shed as a sister engine arrives with a train for Pier Head on Sunday 22 August 1965. Withdrawal for No 21 came on 15 May 1966. *John Corkill*

Above: At Ryde St John's Road station on Saturday 21 August 1965 'O2' Class 0-4-4T No 29 *Alverstone* proceeds light engine towards Pier Head. Withdrawal came for this engine on 1 May 1966. *John Corkill*

Right: 'O2' Class 0-4-4T No 20 *Shanklin* has just arrived at Cowes, with a wet Isle of Wight welcome for passengers and holidaymakers leaving the station on Sunday 22 August 1965. *Shanklin* was withdrawn on 1 January 1967. *John Corkill*

Opposite: Leaving Cowes station for Ryde on Saturday 21 August 1965 is 'O2' class 0-4-4T No 21 *Sandown*. Signs of neglect are now creeping in, with weed-grown sidings and platform surfaces in need of repair. The lines to Cowes closed on 21 February the following year. *John Corkill*

T. GANGE & SONS
COAL & COKE
MERCHANTS

At London's Nine Elms shed on a murky Sunday 22 April 1962, unrebuilt 'West Country' Class 4-6-2 No 34103 *Calstock* is being oiled up ready for duty. It had arrived new from Brighton Works at Stewarts Lane shed, London, in February 1950, and was one of the engines kept in excellent condition for working the 'Golden Arrow' express. In November 1956 it moved to the care of Dover shed, then in January 1961 went to Bournemouth. Its final transfer was to Eastleigh in September 1964, where it was withdrawn on 26 September 1966, and later scrapped.
John Corkill

'Z' Class 0-8-0T No 30956 – with a power classification of 6F – stands at its home shed of Exmouth Junction on Thursday 30 July 1959. This was a Maunsell design, with only eight engines constructed, all at Brighton Works in 1929, with the intention of using them on heavy shunting work. All were withdrawn in November and December 1962; No 30956, the last to remain in service, went on 22 December. By 1 January of that year the whole class had been allocated to Exmouth Junction shed, and were employed as bankers, assisting trains climbing the 1 in 37 gradient between Exeter St David's and Queen Street stations. *Peter Hanson*

Above: Seen at Exmouth Junction shed on 30 July 1959 was 'N15' 'King Arthur' Class 4-6-0 No 30449 *Sir Torre*, which was based at Salisbury and withdrawn six months later on 19 December 1959. This was one of the first batch built at Eastleigh Works, entering traffic in June 1925. They were built to the LSWR loading gauge, which restricted their workings on the Western Section of the Southern. No 30449 was the engine selected to take part in the Darlington Railway Centenary celebrations in 1925, due to the fact that it was the latest express design to appear from Eastleigh Works. *Peter Hanson*

Opposite: 'USA' Class 0-6-0T No 30073 stands at Eastleigh shed in 1966. The 'USA' tanks were a class of 14 engines, purchased in 1946 by the Southern Railway from the USA Army Transportation Corps, having been used during the Second World War. They were all allocated to Southampton Docks until diesel locomotives started to take over, and were then transferred to service stock at Eastleigh shed. One engine, No 30072, became shed pilot at Guildford. No 30073 came to Eastleigh in June 1963 and was withdrawn on 8 January 1967, and later scrapped. Four of the class survive into preservation. *John Corkill*

3F
30073

At Eastleigh Works on Thursday 8 September 1966 'Battle of Britain' Class 4-6-2 No 34089 602 *Squadron* receives a light casual repair. This was the last steam locomotive to be repaired at Eastleigh for normal service, and left the works on 3 October amid press and television publicity. No 34089 was one of those used on the RCTS special to Weymouth seen earlier. *John Corkill*

Being prepared for repainting inside Eastleigh Works on the same day is preserved 'Schools' Class 4-4-0 No 30926 *Repton*. New to Bournemouth shed from Eastleigh in June 1934, it was withdrawn from Basingstoke shed on 30 December 1962. *John Corkill*

At Liverpool Lime Street station on 28 July 1962 'Princess Coronation' Class 4-6-2 No 46234 *Duchess of Abercorn* is about to leave with a Saturday afternoon relief working for London Euston. Locomotives for this duty would work in on Friday evening, bringing a variety of 'Pacifics' to Liverpool, including No 46234, which was allocated to Carlisle Upperby, remaining there until withdrawn during the week ended 26 January 1963. *John Corkill*

Right: 'Royal Scot' Class 4-6-0 No 46120 *Royal Inniskilling Fusilier* receives attention from local train enthusiasts at Lime Street on Saturday 31 December 1960 as it prepares to leave on an early afternoon express to London Euston. Allocated to Camden shed, it moved to Willesden in January 1961, and Llandudno Junction shed eight months later. Final transfer was to Crewe North in June 1963, with withdrawal coming during the week ended 6 July 1963. *John Corkill*

Left: Another 'Royal Scot' 4-6-0, No 46144 *Honourable Artillery Company*, gets to grips with a mid-afternoon service from Lime Street station to North Wales on Saturday 3 November 1962. Allocated to Llandudno Junction, where it had been maintained since transfer from Willesden shed in September 1961, this engine joined the Crewe North allocation in June 1963 and survived until the week ended 11 January 1964. *John Corkill*

Opposite: Stanier 5MT 4-6-0 No 44738 leaves Lime Street station on Saturday 9 June 1962 with an express for Llandudno. This was one of 20 in the class that were fitted with Caprotti valve gear and low running plates, giving them a very different appearance from other class members. No 44738 was a Llandudno Junction-based engine until transferred to Liverpool's Speke Junction shed in November 1963. Withdrawal came during the week ended 6 June 1964. *John Corkill*

44738

47487

Left: On Saturday 3 November 1962 ex-LMS 3F 0-6-0T No 47487 was needed to remove English Electric Type 4 (later Class 40) diesel locomotive No D215 *Aquitania* from an early afternoon departure to London Euston, after the diesel failed with low coolant level due to the failure of a water pump seal. The train left more than 40 minutes late, with one of Edge Hill's Stanier 'Pacifics' in charge. No 47487 had been transferred to Edge Hill from Devons Road, London, during the week ended 30 December 1950, and stayed until withdrawn during the week ended 21 August 1965. *John Corkill*

Above ight: 'Jinty' 0-6-0T No 47416, another of the Edge Hill-based engines, removes the non-corridor coaching stock from an earlier arrival at Lime Street station on Saturday 6 April 1963. This locomotive had also come to Edge Hill during 1950, arriving from Crewe South shed during the week ended 29 April, remaining on allocation until withdrawal, which came during the week ended 25 June 1966. *John Corkill*

Right: This atmospheric night scene at Liverpool Lime Street station on Wednesday 16 December 1964 features Rose Grove-allocated Stanier 5MT 4-6-0 No 44894 on a parcels working. This was one of the few booked workings from the station for steam traction at the time. No 44894 lasted in service to the very end of steam, being withdrawn from Carnforth shed during the week ended 10 August 1968. *John Corkill*

THE RED ROSE
46246

Left: 'Princess Coronation' Class 4-6-2 No 46246 *City of Manchester*, a Camden-based locomotive, backs the empty stock of the 'Red Rose' express out of Lime Street's Platform 7 on a Saturday in July 1960, under the careful control of driver 'Snowy' Roberts. No 46246 remained at Camden shed until withdrawal during the week ended 26 January 1963. *John Corkill*

Right: Looking in very good condition on Saturday 14 July 1962, 'Royal Scot' Class 4-6-0 No 46111 *Royal Fusilier*, allocated to Willesden, backs out of Lime Street after having brought in an earlier arrival. No 46111 was transferred to Annesley shed during the week ended 12 January 1963, for working the Nottingham to Marylebone semi-fast trains over the former Great Central route, withdrawal coming during the week ended 28 September 1963. *John Corkill*

Above: Passing Edge Hill station, Liverpool, on Sunday 2 May 1965 is Stanier 5MT 4-6-0 No 45059, a Speke Junction engine, which was deputising for the failed rostered diesel locomotive on this Newcastle train. No 45059 was built at Vulcan Foundry and was first allocated to Crewe North shed on 8 December 1934. It finished its days at Speke Junction, withdrawal coming during the week ended 8 July 1967. *John Corkill*

Below: BR Standard 'Britannia' Class 4-6-2 No 70017 *Arrow* powers away from Liverpool on the Edge Hill curve on Wednesday 27 June 1962 with a trade special for a visit to the Cadbury factory at Bournville. This was an Aston-allocated engine, specially prepared for this duty. It started life on the Western Region at Old Oak Common when new, on 30 June 1951, and moved to Cardiff Canton in December 1956. The London Midland Region acquired it in June 1958 when it transferred to Kentish Town and, after a number of re-allocations, it ended up at Carlisle Kingmoor in May 1966, where during the week ended 1 October 1966 withdrawal came. *John Corkill*

'Princess Coronation' Class 4-6-2 No 46221 *Queen Elizabeth* rounds the Edge Hill curve in the opposite direction, heading towards Lime Street station on Tuesday 17 July 1962. The bridge in the background carried the freight lines to and from the vast 'Grid Iron' marshalling yards as well as the occasional passenger train to Riverside station, on the River Mersey waterfront. No 46221 was, at this time, a Carlisle Upperby-based engine, withdrawal coming during the week ended 18 May 1963. *John Corkill*

Ex-LNWR 'G2' Class 7F 0-8-0 No 49432, on the 'Grid Iron' track, crosses the Liverpool to Manchester line with a freight on Monday 7 May 1962. These workings could be anything up to 50 wagon loads, depending on traffic flow at Spekeland Road goods depot, which was alongside Edge Hill station. The gradient was severe, lasting just over 2 miles to the top of the grid. With engines working at full regulator, the noise could be heard all around the area. No 49432 was based at Nuneaton shed for many years, before transfer to Edge Hill in January 1961; withdrawal came during the week ended 1 December 1962.
John Corkill

Above: Stanier 5MT 4-6-0 No 44906 works a short train of mineral wagons for Bold Colliery close to Edge Hill shed on Tuesday 9 March 1965. Built at Crewe Works, No 44906 entered traffic in October 1945 and came to Edge Hill from Carlisle Upperby during the week ended 25 December 1948. It remained in Liverpool through to withdrawal, which came during the week ended 2 March 1968. *John Corkill*

Right: On Wednesday 2 June 1965 Stanier 5MT 4-6-0 No 45297 works the 11.00am Liverpool-Newcastle service near Edge Hill shed, deputising for a Gateshead diesel locomotive that had failed. Earlier in the day No 45297 had been called in to cover for another failed diesel engine, which should have worked the 12.45am Lime Street to Glasgow overnight train. The 'Black Five' worked as far as Carnforth, then returned on the Glasgow to Lime Street departure, after yet another diesel failure. No 45297 was built by Armstrong Whitworth & Co and went new to Monument Lane shed, Birmingham, on 2 January 1937. When this photograph was taken the engine was based at Crewe South shed, where it had been allocated since transfer from Preston during the week ended 9 September 1961. It remained until withdrawn during the week ended 16 September 1967. *John Corkill*

Below: Stanier 5MT 4-6-0 No 45284, its exhaust highlighted by the evening sunshine, works one of the last steam workings to the top of the 'Grid Iron' sidings on Friday 3 May 1968, with only a few days to go before Edge Hill shed closes. No 45284 was built by Armstrong Whitworth & Co and went into service at Leeds Holbeck in December 1936. It had transferred to Edge Hill from Holyhead during the week ended 28 October 1961. Withdrawal came when it returned to the shed after its duties were completed on 3 May 1968. *John Corkill*

Right: An unidentified Stanier 8F 2-8-0 works a coal train around the circle line, past Engine Shed Junction, Edge Hill, on its way to the 'Grid Iron' in June 1965. The little corner shop advertises a charter on the Cunard liner *Queen Mary* for readers of the popular newspaper *News of the World*. *John Corkill*

NEWS
WORLD
CHARTERS
THE
Queen Mary

At Liverpool Exchange station in June 1967 Stanier 5MT 4-6-0 No 44819 waits to leave with a passenger train to Blackpool North. No 44819 had been transferred to Wigan Springs Branch shed from Warrington Dallam the previous month, and was withdrawn during the week ended 2 December 1967. Liverpool Exchange station closed on 30 April 1977. *John Corkill*

Stanier 5MT 4-6-0 No 45312 is also awaiting departure from Liverpool Exchange with a working to Blackpool North in mid-July 1963. Note the classic motorbike and sidecar on the otherwise deserted platform. Although still showing a painted 8F Wigan Springs Branch shed code, No 45312 had been transferred to Edge Hill during the week ended 6 July 1963, and awaits the fitting of its 8A shed plate. It moved to Warrington Dallam in February 1966, then Stockport Edgeley in October 1967, and finally Bolton in May 1968. Withdrawal came during the week ended 29 June 1968. *John Corkill*

'Princess Coronation' Class 4-6-2 No 46243 *City of Lancaster* arrives at Liverpool Exchange with an express from Glasgow during the early evening of Saturday 21 July 1962. No 46243 had worked to Glasgow on the 12.45am from Liverpool Lime Street that morning, and worked back to Liverpool on the 9.43am departure from Glasgow. This became a regular working for the Stanier 'Pacifics' based at Edge Hill shed, requiring a high standard of maintenance for these engines and resulting in some useful work from them during their last years in service. No 46243 had come to Edge Hill from Camden during the week ended 11 March 1961, together with Nos 46229 and 46241 from Crewe North, all three remaining on allocation until withdrawn during 1964; *City of Lancaster* was taken out of service during the week ended 12 September. *John Corkill*

Left: Although by 1964 there were plenty of diesel multiple units available, there was still work for 2-6-4Ts on local passenger trains. This was the situation at Walton Junction on the same day as the previous picture as Stanier 2-6-4T No 42626 heads a stopping passenger train to Liverpool Exchange. This locomotive dated from August 1938 and had been built at Derby Works. When this scene was recorded it was allocated to Bolton shed, where it had been since October 1952; it remained there until withdrawal during the week ended 23 October 1965. *John Corkill*

Right: At Walton Junction, Liverpool, BR Standard 4MT 4-6-0 No 75048, allocated to Liverpool Bank Hall, passes by with a Liverpool Exchange to Manchester Exchange passenger train on Saturday 15 August 1964. This engine was one of the batch built at Swindon Works and was first allocated to Accrington shed, during the week ended 24 October 1953. Withdrawal came at the very end of steam, when allocated to Carnforth shed. Its last duties were on the Ulverston shunt, leaving Carnforth at 7.53am and returning in the early afternoon. It was noted every day during the week ended 19 July, its final run on this duty being on 1 August 1968. *John Corkill*

East Princes
45305

Left: On Saturday 6 April 1968 The Locomotive Club of Great Britain ran a tour named 'The Lancastrian'. It started at Liverpool Lime Street, and followed a route taking in Warrington, Stockport, Manchester, Wigan and Southport, then back to Lime Street via Liverpool Riverside. Here we see the tour leaving Riverside station, passing East Princes Dock, with Edge Hill-allocated Stanier 5MT 4-6-0 No 45305 in charge. When Edge Hill closed in 1968, No 45305 transferred to Lostock Hall shed and remained active through to the last day of BR steam. *John Corkill*

Below: 'Royal Scot' Class 4-6-0 No 46123 *Royal Irish Fusilier*, on an express bound for Liverpool on Saturday 13 June 1959, passes Mossley Hill station, nearly 4 miles out from Lime Street. No 46123 was an Edge Hill engine at the time and moved to Kentish Town shed three months later. In June 1961 it was transferred to Saltley shed, Birmingham, and a year later went north to Carlisle Upperby. Withdrawal came during the week ended 3 November 1962. *Peter Hanson*

Stanier 2-6-4T No 42549 has stopped at Mossley Hill station on a local for Liverpool Lime Street on 13 June 1959. This was a Manchester Newton Heath engine and looks in good condition. Withdrawal came from its Manchester depot during the week ended 18 November 1961. *Peter Hanson*

Leaving Mossley Hill station with a stopping train for Lime Street on Saturday 27 February 1960 is Stanier 5MT 4-6-0 No 44735. Added to stock under British Railways, No 44735 was first allocated to Newton Heath shed at the beginning of March 1949, after construction at Crewe Works. Its first transfer was to Trafford Park in mid-November 1964, returning to Newton Heath in March 1968. The final move was to Carnforth, when Newton Heath closed to steam on 1 July 1968, and withdrawal came at the end of steam one month later. *Peter Hanson*

'Jubilee' Class 4-6-0 No 45670 *Howard of Effingham* leaves Mossley Hill on the 5.15pm Crewe to Liverpool train on Wednesday 13 April 1960. This was an Edge Hill-allocated engine, which had come to the shed from Patricroft shed, Manchester, in October 1949. During the week ended 11 June 1960, it was transferred to Crewe North, then on to Willesden, Rugby and Derby, before going to Stockport Edgeley during the week ended 26 September 1964. By this time it may have been in poor condition, as it was withdrawn one month later. *Peter Hanson*

'Princess Coronation' Class 4-6-2 No 46234 *Duchess of Abercorn* passes the site of Wavertree station, Liverpool, which closed on 5 August 1958, with the 'Crewe local' to Lime Street on Saturday 16 April 1960. This route was used as a running-in turn for locomotives that had received overhauls at Crewe Works. No 46234 had been released from the works on 13 April after a heavy intermediate repair, eventually returning to its home shed of Carlisle Upperby. Withdrawal came during the week ended 26 January 1963. *Peter Hanson*

Llandudno Junction-based 'Jubilee' Class 4-6-0 No 45586 *Mysore* leaves Allerton on a local stopping train on Thursday 14 April 1960. This was originally the Cheshire Lines Committee route into Liverpool, from Warrington and Manchester, and the old CLC ten-road engine shed can be seen in the background. This closed in 1897, but continued in use as a wagon repair centre and carriage cleaning facility. It finally closed in the mid-1960s and was eventually demolished. No 45586's final allocation was Crewe South shed, withdrawal coming during the week ended 23 January 1965. *Peter Hanson*

Stanier 5MT 4-6-0 No 44695 passes Kirkby Station signal box with a Liverpool to Bradford express on Saturday 27 June 1959. This was the old Lancashire & Yorkshire Railway route from Liverpool, through Rainford and Wigan. When released from Horwich Works as a new engine, No 44695 was first allocated to Bradford Low Moor shed and had been there since December 1950. It remained until April 1964, when it transferred to Mirfield, only to return to Low Moor in November 1966, and was withdrawn during the week ended 17 June 1967. *Peter Hanson*

Below: 'Royal Scot' Class 4-6-0 No 46156 *The South Wales Borderer*, allocated to Edge Hill, passes Broad Green station on the line out to St Helens on a diverted Sunday working, the 10.00am Liverpool Lime Street to London train, on 31 May 1959. No 46156 was another of the 'Royal Scot' locomotives that finished its working life on the old Great Central main line; it was transferred to Annesley shed in October 1963, and withdrawn during the week ended 10 October 1964. *Peter Hanson*

Right: On Sunday 5 March 1967, the last steam-hauled passenger trains from Birkenhead Woodside station and through services to and from London Paddington ended. Two specials worked in during the day to mark the occasion, one hauled by 'Castle' Class 4-6-0 No 7029 *Clun Castle*, and the second by immaculately turned-out Stanier 5MT 4-6-0 No 44680. While these locomotives were being serviced at Birkenhead shed, the two specials ran to Chester and back behind specially prepared BR Standard 9F 2-10-0s Nos 92203 and 92234. This photograph shows No 92203 waiting for the first special to arrive. The 9F was withdrawn from Birkenhead shed on 11 November 1967, but was saved for preservation. Alongside is Stanier 2-6-4T No 42616, with red-backed number plate, on station pilot duties. This engine was transferred from Birkenhead to Bradford Low Moor at the end of April 1967, withdrawal coming on 30 September 1967. *John Corkill*

ENHEAD
DSIDE
92203

92234
8H
92234

Left: The second 9F 2-10-0 used on the specials, No 92234, awaits the arrival of its train. This engine had entered traffic on 19 August 1958 at Pontypool Road shed after being built at Crewe Works. It was withdrawn on 11 November 1967 from Birkenhead shed, after a very short working life. *John Corkill*

Right: 'Jubilee' Class 4-6-0 No 45552 *Silver Jubilee* leaves Wigan North Western station with a northbound express on Saturday 1 August 1964. The first of the class to be built, as No 5552, it emerged from Crewe Works on 1 December 1934 and was allocated to Crewe North shed. With 1935 being the Silver Jubilee of the reign of King George V and Queen Mary, the opportunity was taken not only to name an engine in honour of the occasion, but also to dedicate the name to the class as a whole, so that was why this locomotive, first of the class, was chosen. The original No 5552 swapped identities with No 5642 on 24 April 1935 while in Crewe Works, and remained so for the rest of its working life. The 'Silver Jubilee' nameplates were added on 17 May 1935 in raised chrome-finish letters, together with similar cabside numbers and 'LMS' on the tender. Withdrawal came during the week ended 26 September 1964 from Crewe North shed. *John Corkill*

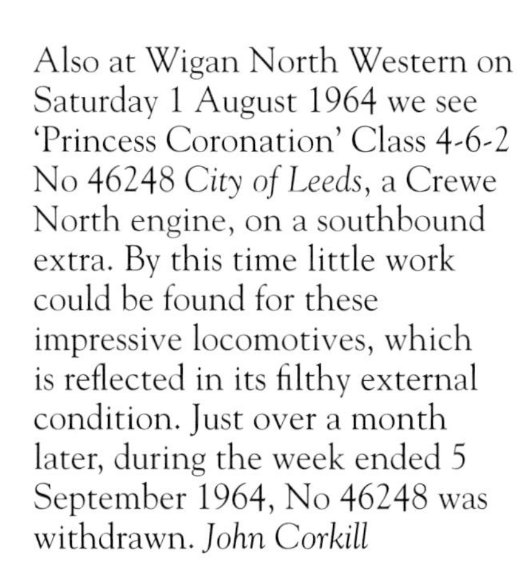

Also at Wigan North Western on Saturday 1 August 1964 we see 'Princess Coronation' Class 4-6-2 No 46248 *City of Leeds*, a Crewe North engine, on a southbound extra. By this time little work could be found for these impressive locomotives, which is reflected in its filthy external condition. Just over a month later, during the week ended 5 September 1964, No 46248 was withdrawn. *John Corkill*

On Friday 19 August 1966 Stanier 5MT 4-6-0 No 44863 heads north with a freight at Boars Head Bank, north of Wigan, on the main line to Preston, with new semi-detached houses in the background. No 44863 was an Edge Hill engine that had transferred from Bletchley during the week ended 10 July 1965; it remained there until withdrawal during the week ended 6 May 1967. *John Corkill*

left: Also seen at Boars Head Bank on the same day was Stanier 5MT 4-6-0 No 44795, tackling the grade with a train of Presflo cement wagons. This locomotive had been built at Horwich Works in August 1947 and was allocated to Carlisle Kingmoor for its entire working life, withdrawal coming during the week ended 29 July 1967. *John Corkill*

Right: On Wednesday 29 April 1959 'Princess Coronation' Class 4-6-2 No 46251 *City of Nottingham*, allocated to Crewe North and heading an afternoon London to Glasgow express, approaches the site of Preston Brook station, which closed on 1 March 1948 and was situated south of Warrington on the West Coast Main Line. No 46251 had been involved in the Winsford crash on Saturday 17 April 1948, when 'Princess Royal' Class 4-6-2 No 6207, heading a Glasgow express, had been stopped by an illicit pull of the communication cord. No 6251 entered the section while working a mail train and ploughed into the rear of the passenger train, resulting in the loss of 24 lives. The accident was blamed on a signalling error. No 46251 was withdrawn from Crewe North shed during the week ended 12 September 1964. *Peter Hanson*

London Midland Region

Preston

Entering Preston station on a northbound express in May 1967 is Carlisle Kingmoor-allocated BR Standard 'Britannia' Class 4-6-2 No 70022, with its *Tornado* nameplates removed. New to traffic on 16 August 1951, its first allocation was Plymouth Laira shed. In September 1961 it came under LMR control by being allocated to Carlisle Kingmoor, followed by a series of transfers, including Longsight, Aston, Rugby and Upperby. No 70022 returned to Kingmoor in December 1966, and was withdrawn on 23 December 1967. *John Corkill*

Stanier 5MT 4-6-0 No 44822, allocated to Newton Heath shed, Manchester, enters Preston from the south in May 1967 with a passenger train. The semaphore signals, signal box and water column all add to the scene, now all swept away in today's modern railway infrastructure. No 44822 survived at Newton Heath until withdrawal during the week ended 21 October 1967. *John Corkill*

Below: Passing by the west side of Preston station on a northbound freight in May 1967 is Stanier 5MT 4-6-0 No 44674. Built at Horwich Works, the engine came into traffic on 9 March 1950 and was allocated to Carlisle Kingmoor. It remained there throughout its life, apart from a short period in 1964 when Lostock Hall shed acquired it. Withdrawal came on 30 December 1967, the same day as Carlisle Kingmoor shed closed. *John Corkill*

Opposite top: Stanier 8F 2-8-0 No 48252, with a painted 6C code (for Croes Newydd shed, Wrexham) gently runs north through Preston with a partially fitted freight in May 1967. In June it moved to Crewe South, then in August to Heaton Mersey, withdrawal coming during the week ended 4 May 1968. *John Corkill*

Right: Stanier 5MT 4-6-0 No 44942, allocated to Lostock Hall shed, runs south on the western side of Preston station with a train of mineral wagons in June 1967. No 44942 was another Horwich-built locomotive dating from December 1945. After spending many years allocated to Aston, withdrawal came during the week ended 22 June 1968 from Lostock Hall. *John Corkill*

On Tuesday 16 July 1968 Stanier 'Black Five' 4-6-0 No 45017, a Carnforth engine, heads north past Preston station with a van train. This was the oldest of the class still active at the time. Built at Crewe Works, it entered service on 16 May 1935, and was first allocated to Inverness. From August 1951 to May 1959 it spent time at Carnforth, then wandered between allocations at Wigan Springs Branch, Southport, Newton Heath and Trafford Park, before returning to Carnforth during August 1965. Chalked on the smokebox door is 'I am a good engine, please preserve me'. Sadly this was not to be, as withdrawal for this locomotive came at the very end of steam in 1968. *John Corkill*

Passing on the east side of Preston station in June 1967 is BR Standard 'Britannia' Class 4-6-2 No 70045 *Lord Rowallan*, minus nameplates, on a southbound parcels train. No 70045 entered traffic on 16 June 1954 at Holyhead shed and stayed until November 1959, when it was transferred to Crewe North. A succession of sheds followed until it returned to Holyhead in December 1962. During a visit to Crewe Works for a light casual repair in February 1965, it was fitted with LMS-style oval-headed buffers, after collision damage. In June of that year No 70045 went to Oxley shed, Wolverhampton, then four months later to Banbury, and finally to Carlisle Kingmoor at the beginning of January 1966. Withdrawal came on 30 December 1967. *John Corkill*

In seemingly good condition in June 1967, Stanier 5MT 4-6-0 No 45345 heads a southbound parcels train on the east side of Preston station, with its 10D Lostock Hall shed code chalked on the smokebox. This engine was one of the many built by Armstrong Whitworth & Co for the LMS, and went new to Carnforth shed on 17 April 1937. It spent its entire career working from sheds in the North West and North Wales, and withdrawal came from Lostock Hall during the week ended 25 May 1968. *John Corkill*

HOTEL

Left: Stanier 5MT 4-6-0 No 44926 arrives at the north end of Preston station with a passenger train from Blackpool on Sunday 29 July 1962. In the background is a selection of classic cars in the taxi rank, and a moped and scooter on the platform. No 44926 was built at Crewe Works in February 1946 and moved from Southport shed to Blackpool in April 1952, staying until September 1964, when it transferred to Bolton. Later allocations saw it at Patricroft, Newton Heath, Lancaster, and finally Edge Hill shed in April 1966, withdrawal coming during the week ended 20 April 1968. *John Corkill*

Below left: Saturday 20 April 1968 was the day the RCTS organised the 'Lancastrian No 2' rail tour from Liverpool Lime Street, using a variety of steam locomotives and routes. Part of the trip was from Fleetwood to Preston hauled by BR Standard 'Britannia' Class 4-6-2 No 70013 *Oliver Cromwell*, which used various junctions in order to arrive at Preston facing north, allowing the train to go to Oxenholme for a run down the Windermere branch. This was the scene at Preston with No 70013 awaiting departure, with inspector Donald Norman of Edge Hill, complete with bowler hat, on the footplate. *John Corkill*

Opposite: At the north end of Preston station, also in June 1967, an unidentified 'Black Five' enters with an extra passenger working, as a 'Ribble' double-decker bus passes over the bridge. *John Corkill*

Right: This photograph was taken from the 'Lancastrian No 2' rail tour train leaving Preston for the Windermere branch, passing Stanier 5MT 4-6-0 No 45156 *Ayrshire Yeomanry*, which had worked part of the tour from Liverpool. This is the north end of Preston station, which was graced by the impressive signal gantry. *John Corkill*

London Midland Region

Carlisle and Crewe

At Carlisle Citadel station, Ivatt 2MT 2-6-2T No 41222 is the south end station pilot, shunting milk tankers on Saturday 13 February 1965. Built at Crewe Works, No 41222 was first allocated to Crewe North during the week ended 2 October 1948, no doubt for running-in purposes, as two weeks later the engine was sent to Bangor shed. During August 1949 it was transferred to Bletchley, where it stayed until the beginning of January 1965, when it moved to Carlisle Upperby. When the latter shed closed on 12 December 1966, No 41222 was transferred to Carlisle Kingmoor and probably not used, as withdrawal came during the last week of that month. *John Corkill*

Right: At the north end of Carlisle Citadel station, 'Princess Coronation' Class 4-6-2 No 46257 *City of Salford* is ready to depart with the 9.43am Liverpool Exchange to Glasgow train on Sunday 2 September 1962. No 46257 was the last of the class to be built, entering traffic after nationalisation at Camden shed on 22 May 1948. In September 1958 the engine was transferred to Carlisle Upperby, then in March 1961 to Carlisle Kingmoor. Withdrawal came during the week ended 12 September 1964. *John Corkill*

Left: Arriving at Carlisle Citadel station from the south with a heavy parcels train on Sunday 29 July 1962 is 'Royal Scot' Class 4-6-0 No 46123 *Royal Irish Fusilier* piloting 'Jubilee' Class 4-6-0 No 45558 *Manitoba*. No 46123 was allocated to Carlisle Upperby, from where it was withdrawn during the week ended 3 November 1962. The 'Jubilee' was based at Manchester Patricroft, then was transferred to Leeds Holbeck during the week ended 25 April 1964, followed by what was probably a 'paper move' only during the week ended 15 August to Newton Heath, Manchester, as the engine was withdrawn during the same week. *John Corkill*

'Princess Coronation' Class 4-6-2 No 46256 *Sir William A. Stanier F.R.S.* stands at Crewe on the RCTS 'Scottish Lowlander' special on Saturday 26 September 1964, awaiting departure. At the time this 'Pacific' was the last survivor of the class, and had been retained in service to work the tour for what was to be the engine's last run. The other 16 class members had been withdrawn during the week ended 12 September. The special left Crewe at 9.15am and ran to Carlisle, where 'A4' 4-6-2 No 60007 *Sir Nigel Gresley* took over for a run over the Waverley route to Niddrie West Junction; another 'A4' 4-6-2, No 60009 *Union of South Africa*, then became the motive power. The tour then ran over the Edinburgh suburban line through to Glasgow, over the Glasgow & South Western line through Kilmarnock and Dumfries, then back to Carlisle. From Carlisle south to Crewe No 46256 took over the train for its last passenger duty; withdrawal from Crewe North shed followed during the week ended 3 October 1964. *John Corkill*

At Crewe station on Saturday 13 February 1965 the south end pilot duties are in the hands of ex-LMS 3F 0-6-0T No 47450, seen here in the south end bay platform. Dating from July 1927, No 47450 had been built by Hunslet Engine Co to the LMS design. Crewe South acquired the 'Jinty' from Birkenhead in November 1949, and it stayed on allocation until withdrawal during the week ended 2 April 1966. *John Corkill*

Left: 'Jinty' 0-6-0T No 47677, a Crewe South engine, is on carriage shunting duties on Sunday 11 December 1960, its clean condition the result of a visit to Derby Works the previous October for repair and overhaul. The locomotive had been transferred to Crewe South shed from Birkenhead during the week ended 28 May 1960, and remained until withdrawal during the week ended 6 November 1965. *John Corkill*

Left: Crewe North-allocated 'Princess Coronation' Class 4-6-2 No 46253 *City of St Albans* rounds the curve past Crewe South shed with a train for Shrewsbury on Sunday 30 October 1960. On Sundays this duty was performed by a variety of engines, dependent on availability at the shed. No 46253 was withdrawn during the week ended 26 January 1963. *John Corkill*

Ex-LNWR 'G2A' Class 7F 0-8-0 No 49002, also seen on Sunday 30 October 1960, is just off the works at Crewe South shed and awaits return to its Nuneaton home. Transfer to Edge Hill came during January 1961, then to Wigan Springs Branch in September of that year, from where withdrawal came during the week ended 15 September 1962. *John Corkill*

Crewe Works

On Sunday 12 April 1959 a line-up of Stanier 5MT 4-6-0s is seen in the yard at Crewe Works, with No 45195, allocated to Bletchley, in the middle, after receiving a heavy intermediate overhaul. Built by Armstrong Whitworth & Co, it entered traffic on 12 October 1935 and operated from 16 different depots, with Carlisle Kingmoor shed its final destination in October 1963, withdrawal coming during the week ended 30 July 1966. *Peter Hanson*

Stanier 8F 2-8-0 No 48764 was photographed outside the paint shop on the same day, ready to return to Willesden shed, London. The engine's final allocation was Bolton, arriving during the week ended 9 December 1967; it was withdrawn the following week. *Peter Hanson*

At Crewe Works on Sunday 30 October 1960 BR Standard 'Britannia' Class 4-6-2 No 70015 *Apollo* has received classified repairs and attention to the boiler tubes. It then returned to Trafford Park shed and did not visit the works again until January 1965, when a heavy intermediate overhaul was carried out. Carlisle Kingmoor was *Apollo*'s last allocation, from where withdrawal came during the week ended 5 August 1967. Alongside are the frames and other parts of Standard 2-6-2T No 84011.After this works visit the complete engine returned to Lower Darwen. It's last allocation had been Fleetwood, from March 1961, where it remained until withdrawal during the week ended 24 April 1965. *John Corkill*

On that same Sunday, some finishing touches are being applied to 'Jubilee' Class 4-6-0 No 45650 *Blake* outside the Erecting Shop at Crewe Works, after a heavy intermediate overhaul. Allocated to Leicester Midland shed at the time, the engine was one of the class transferred to Burton-on-Trent in November 1961 and withdrawn during the week ended 19 January 1963. *John Corkill*

Right: Also seen at the works on 30 October 1960 is another 'Jubilee', No 45602 *British Honduras*, outside the Paint Shop after a heavy general repair. Returning to Sheffield Millhouses shed, the locomotive was later transferred to Leeds Holbeck, where withdrawal came on 18 March 1965. *John Corkill*

Left: At Crewe Works on Tuesday 20 March 1962 is unrebuilt 'Patriot' Class 4-6-0 No 45504 *Royal Signals*; it had been withdrawn from Bristol Barrow Road shed the previous week. Allocated to Barrow Road during the week ended 15 November 1958 together with Nos 45506 and 45519, it was the first time this type of engine had been based there in British Railways days. All three locomotives were withdrawn at the same time and the trio were all present together at Crewe on this day, ready for scrapping three days later. *John Corkill*

A visit to Crewe Works on Friday 13 April 1962 finds 'Princess Royal' Class 4-6-2 No 46205 *Princess Victoria* awaiting scrapping after withdrawal from Willesden shed during the week ended 25 November 1961. This was the only one of the class to have a different set of valve gear, with a modified large motion bracket fitted in 1938, some three years after being built. *John Corkill*

North Eastern and Scottish Regions

Miscellany

At York station on Saturday 23 June 1962 a young enthusiast watches King's Cross-allocated 'A4' Class 4-6-2 No 60032 *Gannet* arrive on a southbound express. When King's Cross shed closed on 16 June 1963 No 60032 moved to Peterborough New England; withdrawal came on 20 October of that year. *John Corkill*

BR Standard 9F 2-10-0 No 92187 runs into York station from the north with a parcels train on Saturday 15 July 1961. Built at Swindon Works, the 9F entered traffic at New England shed on 12 February 1958. It transferred to Grantham in June 1958, was back at New England three months later, then finally moved to Colwick, Nottingham, on 9 June 1963. Withdrawal came on 21 February 1965. *John Corkill*

At the level crossing at Goole on Saturday 8 October 1966 the traffic is held up as 'Austerity' 2-8-0 No 90076, a Wakefield engine, runs past light engine. The adverts in the background promote Worthington's beer and cigarettes, and there are some interesting vehicles on view, including a Comet Radiovision Services van, a Ford Anglia, and a moped rider without a crash helmet. No 90076 transferred to Normanton shed in June 1967 and West Hartlepool the following month. Withdrawal came later that year, on 9 September. *John Corkill*

Above: 'J27' Class 0-6-0 No 65894 waits for the signals near Newcastle on Saturday 3 June 1967. This class was a development of a William Worsdell design, with 115 locomotives constructed between 1906 and 1923. No 65894 was the last to be built, entering traffic on 19 September 1923 as LNER No 2392. Withdrawal came on 9 September 1967 from Sunderland shed. Being one of the last surviving members of the class, the engine was saved for preservation by the North East Locomotive Group. *John Corkill*

Right: BR Standard 5MT 4-6-0 No 73154, in excellent condition, leaves Glasgow Buchanan Street station in August 1965 with a train for Stirling. No 73154 was one of 30 of the class fitted with Caprotti valve gear. A batch of ten, Nos 73145 to 73154, were allocated to Glasgow St Rollox shed from new. Built at Derby Works, No 73154 entered traffic on 14 June 1957 and transferred to Stirling shed on 21 December 1965. It finally moved to Motherwell on 13 June 1966 and was withdrawn six months later. *John Corkill*

Below: At Glasgow Central station in August 1965, 'Jubilee' Class 4-6-0 No 45697 *Achilles* is at the stop blocks after working in from Carlisle. The yellow stripe on the cabside was to remind crews that the locomotive must not work south of Crewe, as the electrification wires were lower than those further north. No 45697 was a Leeds Holbeck engine and was withdrawn on 5 September 1967. *John Corkill*

73154

Below: At Buchanan Street station in August 1965, another 'A4', No 60034 *Lord Faringdon*, awaits departure with a fast 3-hour express to Aberdeen. No 60034 came to Scotland from New England shed, Peterborough, in October 1963, transferring to Edinburgh St Margarets, then moved to Aberdeen Ferryhill in May 1964, with withdrawal coming on 24 August 1966. Alongside is one of the St Rollox-allocated Caprotti-fitted BR Standard 5MT 4-6-0s, No 73147, which spent time at this Glasgow shed from new on 13 February 1957 until withdrawal on 21 August 1965. Buchanan Street station closed on 7 November 1966, with services transferred to Queen Street. *John Corkill*

Above: 'A4' Class 4-6-2 No 60027 *Merlin* stands at Glasgow Buchanan Street on Tuesday 7 August 1962 awaiting departure on the 8.25am 'St Mungo' 3-hour express to Aberdeen. No 60027 entered traffic at Edinburgh's Haymarket shed on 13 March 1937 as LNER No 4486, and stayed until displaced by 'Deltic' diesels. It transferred to Glasgow St Rollox on 20 May 1962 for working the Aberdeen trains. Final transfer was back to Edinburgh on 6 September 1964, but this time to St Margarets shed, where withdrawal came on 3 September 1965. *John Corkill*

Left At Perth station on Friday 11 August 1961, 'Princess Coronation' Class 4-6-2 No 46226 *Duchess of Norfolk* is impatient to be away with a southbound express. Allocated to Carlisle Kingmoor, the 'Duchess' was withdrawn during the week ended 12 September 1964. *John Corkill*

Right Stanier 5MT 4-6-0 No 45359 calls at Larbert station on Saturday 18 May 1963 with a local train from Glasgow to Stirling. Built by Armstrong Whitworth & Co, No 45359 was released from the works on 15 May 1937 and started work at Inverness shed. It transferred in June 1943 to Glasgow St Rollox, then to Stirling in November 1948. Its final allocation was Motherwell in June 1966, from where withdrawal came on 1 May 1967. *John Corkill*

Hughes/Fowler 'Crab' 2-6-0 No 42736 passes Kilmarnock station with a brake van on its way to work a coal train on Wednesday 7 July 1965. There was a concentration of these locomotives at the local sheds at Hurlford and Ayr, with 20 of the class distributed between the two locations in 1965. No 42736 dated from February 1927 and was first allocated to Crewe South. In August 1942 it was transferred to Scotland, from Carlisle Kingmoor to Grangemouth. Then in November 1961 the 'Crab' moved to Ayr, and in May 1963 arrived at Hurlford shed. Withdrawal came on 29 November 1966. *John Corkill*

Running through Ayr station on the same day is another 'Crab' 2-6-0, No 42919, with a train of empty coal wagons. Built in November 1930, the engine's final allocation was Ayr shed, withdrawal coming on 27 October 1966. *John Corkill*

On Saturday 23 June 1962 'A2' Class 4-6-2 No 60526 *Sugar Palm* takes a rest inside the roundhouses at York shed. Allocated new to York on 9 January 1948, the engine remained there throughout, apart from between 18 January and 26 September 1948, when it was at Leeds Neville Hill shed. Withdrawal came from York on 12 November 1962. *John Corkill*

In another view inside York motive power depot on the same day we see 'A1' Class 4-6-2 No 60124 *Kenilworth* (left), 'K1' Class 2-6-0 No 62065, and 'B1' Class 4-6-0 No 61229, all allocated to York. No 60124 moved to Darlington shed in November 1964 and final withdrawal came on 27 March 1966. No 62065 remained at York until withdrawn on 20 March 1967, and No 61229 was condemned at York on 29 June 1964. *John Corkill*

Outside the repair shop at York shed, also on 23 June 1962, is York-allocated 'B16' Class 4-6-0 No 61418. This was a Vincent Raven design and entered traffic in November 1920. From a class of 79 engines, seven were rebuilt by Gresley and 17 by Thompson. No 61418 was one of the Thompson rebuilds, carried out in 1944, resulting in three independent sets of Walschaerts valve gear, higher running plates and a longer boiler. As LNER No 921, the engine arrived at York shed from Hull Dairycoates on 1 June 1940, with final transfer back to Dairycoates on 2 December 1962. Withdrawal came on 29 June 1964. *John Corkill*

This is Glasgow Eastfield shed on Thursday 10 August 1961, and 'N15' Class 0-6-2T No 69212 is on shed with the coaling plant in the background. The 'N15' was a Reid design for the North British Railway, and No 69212 spent all its working life in Glasgow. Built at Cowlairs Works, it went new to Glasgow Parkhead shed on 12 December 1923, and its only transfer was to Eastfield on 17 June 1957. Withdrawal came on 1 October 1962, with cutting-up carried out at Cowlairs. *John Corkill*

Edinburgh St Margarets was a six-road straight shed opened in 1866, and situated 1½ miles east of Waverley station. On view on an August day in 1965 is Perth-allocated Stanier 5MT 4-6-0 No 44925. Later in the year, during the week ended 2 October, the engine transferred to St Margarets and remained there until withdrawn on 2 September 1966. St Margarets shed closed on 1 May 1967 and was demolished, part of the site being utilised for the Meadow Bank stadium. *John Corkill*

'Y9' Class 0-4-0ST No 68095 was at Edinburgh St Margarets shed on Friday 11 August 1961. It is standing on the site of the original shed on the opposite side of the main line from the later six-road shed, and was a stone-built roundhouse opened in 1846. By 1944, following a fire, it was virtually derelict and was demolished, the short spurs from the turntable being retained for stabling small tank engines and later diesel shunters. No 68095 was one of a class of 38 engines dating from 1882, with 33 surviving into British Railways ownership. No 68095 had been built at Cowlairs Works and entered service in December 1887. It became the last of the class to be withdrawn on 29 December 1962, and was sold into private ownership for preservation. *John Corkill*

Edge Hill motive power depot was situated in a maze of lines east of Edge Hill station. *The British Locomotive Shed Directory*, published in 1947, gives the following directions: 'Turn right outside Edge Hill station along Tunnel Road. Turn right into Wavertree Road, changing to Picton Road. Turn left into Tiverton Road just past a railway over-bridge. A cinder path leads through a tunnel from the end of this road to the shed. Walking time 15 minutes.' If you wanted to travel out from the city centre you needed to board a No 4 (Penny Lane), 4A (Childwall) or 4W (Woolton) tram and alight at Tiverton Road.

The original shed buildings dated from 1865, and in 1902 they were enlarged when a new structure was built at the rear, extending a number of the through roads. This was known as the 'new' shed and was re-roofed in 1944, the 'old' shed having been dealt with six years earlier. The coaling plant dated from 1914 and was a unique structure built in ferro-concrete with an unusual design, the wagons being propelled along a ramp (a spur from an existing raised line) to discharge directly into the bunkers. New ash plants were installed in 1934 and a water-softening plant in 1938. Coded 8A by the LMS, this was retained through to closure. At nationalisation on 1 January 1948 the allocation was 117 steam locomotives, and on the day the shed closed, 6 May 1968, this had been reduced to 26 steam engines and 10 diesel shunters.

Above: A view of the 'old' shed on Saturday 20 August 1966. Engines on view include Stanier 8F 2-8-0 No 48536, a recent transfer to Edge Hill from Newton Heath, and Stanier 5MT 4-6-0 No 45156 *Ayrshire Yeomanry*, which had transferred from Warrington Dallam in June 1963. *John Corkill*

Opposite top left: On Thursday 3 June 1965, the 'new' shed is on view, and this part was known as 'the camp' to the staff. Outside are a Stanier 8F 2-8-0 and 'Jubilee' Class 4-6-0 No 45590 *Travancore*, which was allocated to Warrington Dallam and had been re-tubed while at Edge Hill. The engine was withdrawn later that year, during the week ended 11 December. *John Corkill*

Top right: Outside the 'new' shed on Monday 16 July 1962 is Crewe North-allocated 'Princess Coronation' Class 4-6-2 No 46256 *Sir William A. Stanier F.R.S.*. The locomotive is coupled to an English Electric Type 4 diesel (later Class 40), which it had towed back to Crewe for repair after having failed the day before. In the right background is Fowler 2F 0-6-0T No 47166. *John Corkill*

Centre right: A closer view of No 47166, acting as shed pilot on Monday 3 September 1962. Built at Derby Works in December 1928, it had a short wheelbase of only 9ft 6in for working round the tight curves of dock lines. The engine had been transferred to Edge Hill from Bidston during the week ended 8 April 1961, with withdrawal coming during the week ended 11 May 1963. *John Corkill*

Bottom right: 'Princess Royal' Class 4-6-2 No 46208 *Princess Helena Victoria* has had some firebox repairs carried out in 1959, which have required the engine to be brought round to 'the camp' area. No 46208 was transferred to Edge Hill from Crewe North in September 1951 and stayed until withdrawn during the week ended 20 October 1962. *John Corkill*

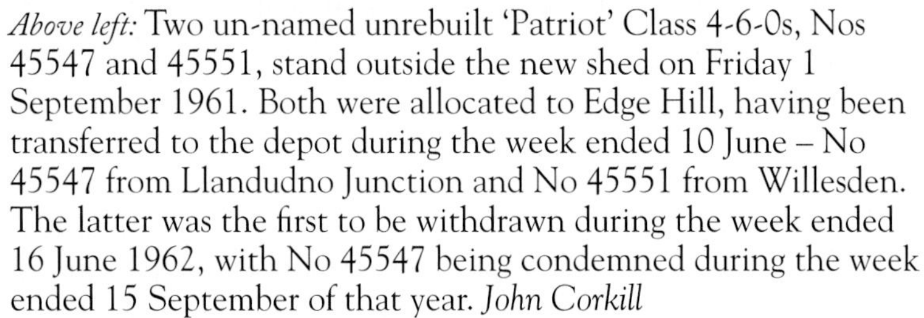

Above left: Two un-named unrebuilt 'Patriot' Class 4-6-0s, Nos 45547 and 45551, stand outside the new shed on Friday 1 September 1961. Both were allocated to Edge Hill, having been transferred to the depot during the week ended 10 June – No 45547 from Llandudno Junction and No 45551 from Willesden. The latter was the first to be withdrawn during the week ended 16 June 1962, with No 45547 being condemned during the week ended 15 September of that year. *John Corkill*

Above right: 'Austerity' 2-8-0s were regular visitors to Edge Hill, and this was the situation on Wednesday 2 June 1965 with No 90573, allocated to Staveley Barrow Hill. Note the higher than normal front number plate. From September 1946 to December 1962 the engine was allocated to GWR and Western Region depots, but during the last week of the latter month it was transferred from Southall to the Eastern Region, at Frodingham. Barrow Hill acquired the locomotive from Canklow in March 1964, with final withdrawal coming during the week ended 15 August 1965. *John Corkill*

Opposite: Wakefield-allocated Austerity 2-8-0 No 90407, seen here in 1966, was another to visit Edge Hill, and will have worked in on a coal train from Yorkshire. No 90407 remained in service until withdrawal during the week ended 3 June 1967. *John Corkill*

90407

HAMPTON GARDENS
44711

Left: At the 'coal hole' at Edge Hill, Stanier 5MT 4-6-0 No 44711 stands alongside Stanier 8F 2-8-0 No 48614 in December 1967, the same month that both engines had joined the allocation. The high-level line can be seen – hopper wagons, with opening bottom doors, are also in view, and were pushed up to replenish the bunkers. Both locomotives had been transferred from Wigan Springs Branch shed and were withdrawn during the week preceding the closure of Edge Hill in 1968. *John Corkill*

Top righte: Being coaled after working in on a freight from Carlisle on Tuesday 26 March 1963 is 'Princess Coronation' Class 4-6-2 No 46233 *Duchess of Sutherland*, with the coaler viewed from the opposite side from that shown in the previous photograph. The locomotive was an Edge Hill engine at the time and was withdrawn on 8 February 1964, but survived into preservation. *John Corkill*

Bottom right: Caprotti-fitted BR Standard 5MT 4-6-0 No 73130, allocated to Manchester Patricroft, has just paid a visit to the coaler on Monday 9 July 1962. New from Derby Works on 12 September 1956, its first allocation was to Shrewsbury. Its only other transfer was to Patricroft, in September 1958, and it was finally withdrawn during the week ended 21 January 1967. *John Corkill*

BR Standard 2MT 2-6-2T No 84000, allocated to Warrington Dallam, makes use of the coaler on Monday 7 May 1962. These locomotives were designed by Riddles for light passenger work, and were the tank engine version of the Standard 2MT 2-6-0 tender engine. No 84000 was the first to be built at Crewe Works and entered traffic during the week ended 4 July 1953 at Crewe North shed. Withdrawal came during the week ended 30 October 1965, from Birkenhead. *John Corkill*

On the 1 in 27 inclined approach road to Edge hill shed on Tuesday 9 March 1965, Stanier 5MT 4-6-0 No 45330, an Aintree engine, passes descending Hughes/Fowler 'Crab' 2-6-0 No 42859, allocated to Birkenhead. This incline tested the skills of drivers when ascending or descending; careful application of the brakes when going down was essential to avoid slipping, especially on wet rails, and travelling up meant a gentle application of the regulator to avoid spinning wheels, which could damage the motion. The bench on the left was for the sander, who would sand the rails of the incline by hand in wet weather conditions, a job usually allotted to an unfortunate cleaner. *John Corkill*

Right: On Monday 4 June 1962 BR Standard 'Britannia' Class 4-6-2 No 70052, without its *Firth of Tay* nameplates, carefully climbs the incline away from the shed on a dry day, so no sander is required. Engine Shed Junction signal box can just be seen in the distance. This 'Britannia' was a Glasgow Corkerhill-allocated engine and was no doubt rostered for a Liverpool Exchange to Glasgow working. Withdrawal came during the week ended 1 April 1967 from Carlisle Kingmoor. *John Corkill*

No 70052 was the locomotive involved in a serious accident on the Settle & Carlisle line on the early morning of Thursday 21 January 1960, when allocated to Glasgow Polmadie, as a result of which five passengers lost their lives and nine were injured. It was one of the rare accidents due to traction equipment failure, and the elements leading to the disaster could be traced back a number of days previously when the right-hand inside slidebar bolt had worked loose. This had been noticed at both Polmadie shed four nights previously and at Leeds Holbeck depot two nights earlier, and in each case it had been tightened. However, on both occasions the split pin was not replaced or a washer inserted under the nut to bring it properly in contact with the split pin. In fact, following a heavy intermediate repair at Crewe Works in September 1959, No 70052's right-hand slidebar bolts had been reported loose at least nine times, but there was no record of them being changed. In the post-accident investigation, expelled motion parts were found on the trackbed in five locations over a distance of 34 miles; these including two bolts that were so worn they should have been replaced.

On the night of the accident No 70052 was heading the eight-coach 9.05pm Glasgow St Enoch to St Pancras train over the Settle & Carlisle line. After Ais Gill driver F. Waites with fireman J. Chester became aware of a serious knocking, and reduced speed. As it got worse the driver stopped at Garsdale in a gale and blizzard to examine his engine as best he could in the darkness and extreme weather conditions. The bearings were cool and the left-hand-side big end, which he suspected was the problem, was in order. However, he did not notice the loss of both right-hand slidebars, which had fallen off earlier, and would have caused the knocking. Instead of proceeding at a slow speed, as there was obviously something wrong, the average speed after Garsdale was around 40mph. With both slidebars gone, the right-hand piston rod sustained severe bending and eventually fractured, together with the union link, with the result that the connecting rod, crosshead and piston rod dropped and were driven 6 feet into the ballast. The connecting rod continued to thrash about and the crosshead thrust hard into the ballast at every wheel revolution. No 70052 was brought to a halt without further harm, but the connecting rod became wedged against the adjacent track, distorting and disrupting the rails.

Shortly afterwards, the northbound 10.40pm Leeds to Carlisle Class H freight, hauled by Carlisle Kingmoor-based Hughes/Fowler 'Crab' 2-6-0 No 42881, appeared, and was derailed on the distorted track, ripping into the passenger train, tearing out the side of the leading coach and five compartments of the third vehicle, and devastating a parcels van. The sleeping cars were not damaged, and in total only 75 passengers were aboard the train.

Prior to this accident other 'Britannia' 'Pacifics' had suffered problems with loose slidebar bolts, with in some instances similar loss or displacement of slidebars, fortunately without serious results. A programme of fixing new front fastenings to cure the loose and failing slidebars had just started, and due to this accident was urgently hastened and expanded to include all 'Britannia' and 'Clan' 4-6-2s as well as BR Standard 5MT 4-6-0s and 9F 2-10-0s. *John Corkill*

Above right: Inside Edge Hill shed on Thursday 3 June 1965, ex-LMS 3F 0-6-0T No 47406 is in steam. This was a relative newcomer to the allocation, having been transferred from Gorton in Manchester during the week ended 23 January. It was withdrawn from Edge Hill during the week ended 24 December 1966, but was later saved for preservation. In the background is Brush Type 2 (later Class 31) diesel locomotive No D5684, which was a Sheffield-based engine and new in January 1961. These diesels had replaced the steam locomotives on freight trains that had for many years been worked by ex-LMS 0-6-0s and 2-8-0s from Grimesthorpe shed. *John Corkill*

Right: 'Royal Scot' Class 4-6-0 No 46115 *Scots Guardsman* takes a rest inside Edge Hill shed before its next duty, which would be the 7.50pm fast goods back to Carlisle on Friday 4 June 1965. Allocated to Carlisle Kingmoor, the engine was withdrawn during the week ended 1 January 1966 and was the last of the class in service. Thankfully, it was preserved and has now been fully restored. *John Corkill*

Right: Stanier 8F 2-8-0 No 48696 sits in the depths of Edge Hill shed during the night of Wednesday 25 January 1967. The engine has the shed code 'Colk' painted on the front, which indicated Colwick, Nottingham, even though that shed had an official code of 16B at the time. The reason for the engine's visit was its transfer from Colwick during the week ended 4 February 1967. It stayed at Edge Hill until withdrawal came during the week ended 30 December of that year. *John Corkill*

Top right: Inside the 'new' shed at Edge Hill on Wednesday 17 April 1968, with a 'Not to be moved' sign attached, is Stanier 5MT 4-6-0 No 45156 *Ayrshire Yeomanry*, being prepared to work part of the RCTS 'Lancastrian No 2' rail tour the following Saturday. The locomotive had been stopped on shed two weeks before the tour to be repainted in the evenings by members of the RCTS Merseyside branch, including John Corkill. The nameplates and number plate were made in wood by Ted Baxendale and the builder's plates borrowed from another Edge Hill 'Black Five', No 45187. *John Corkill*

Bottom right: Recorded on film at around 3.00am on Wednesday 25 January 1967 in the yard at Edge Hill is Sutton Oak-allocated BR Standard 4MT 2-6-0 No 76075. Built at Horwich Works, the engine went new to Sutton Oak on 15 December 1956. Later transfers saw it allocated to Bescot, Stoke-on-Trent, Colwick, and back to Sutton Oak, before finally arriving at Wigan Springs Branch shed in June 1967, from where withdrawal came during the week ended 7 October 1967. *John Corkill*

44711

45156

Page 114: Shed scenes at night evoke a kind of magical atmosphere, and this view in December 1967 shows Stanier 5MT 4-6-0 No 44711 outside the old shed after dark. *John Corkill*

Page 115: Stanier 5MT 4-6-0 No 45156 *Ayrshire Yeomanry* is seen again alongside the coaler in the twilight of the evening after its work on the 'Lancastrian No 2' tour was over. *John Corkill*

Above: Ex-LNWR 'G2' Class 7F 0-8-0 No 49434 stands outside the new shed at Edge Hill on Wednesday 23 May 1962. Dating from August 1922, No 49434 had come to Edge Hill from Birkenhead during the week ended 22 December 1951, and remained on allocation until withdrawal during the week ended 20 October 1962. *John Corkill*

Below: Outside the 'new' shed and out of work on Friday 2 November 1962 is 'G2' No 49448. This view shows in more detail the tender cab that was attached to a number of 'Super Ds' allocated to Edge Hill; they were essential for trips along the Bootle branch, which had a number of tight tunnels at the dock end of the line. No 49448 had transferred to Edge Hill from Sutton Oak during the week ended 10 September 1960, and moved to Crewe South in December 1962, withdrawal coming during the week ended 15 June of the following year. *John Corkill*

BR Standard 'Britannia' Class 4-6-2 No 70020 *Mercury* drops down the 1 in 27 incline at Edge Hill shed on Tuesday 31 July 1962, when allocated to Longsight shed, Manchester. This view shows evidence of the engine's previous career operating on the Western Region – the smoke deflectors have handholds rather than handrails, fitted as a result of the Milton accident of 1955. No 70020 was allocated to Carlisle Kingmoor when withdrawal came during the week ended 21 January 1967. *John Corkill*

Edge Hill never had a 'Standard' 9F 2-10-0 allocated, but they were frequent visitors. This was the case in May 1967 when No 92106 was photographed backing out from the 'coal hole'. The locomotive was a Birkenhead-allocated engine, and was withdrawn during the week ended 29 July 1967. Birkenhead shed was home to a large number of 9Fs, with 68 examples based there from February 1963 until November 1967, when the depot closed. *John Corkill*

Much less frequent visitors to Edge Hill were the 'Standard' 4MT 4-6-0s, but on Thursday 3 June 1965 Aintree-allocated No 75061 has found its way to the shed. New from Swindon Works in May 1957, the engine was first allocated to Leicester Midland, moving to Derby shed in September 1962. In November 1963 it transferred to Walton-on-the-Hill, and a month later to Aintree, where withdrawal came during the week ended 4 February 1967. Edge Hill only ever had one BR Standard locomotive on allocation, 4MT 4-6-0 No 75060, which came from Aintree in June 1965 and left for Croes Newydd, Wrexham, in May 1966. *John Corkill*

'Princess Royal' Class 4-6-2 No 46208 *Princess Helena Victoria* was on shed on Wednesday 25 January 1961, and facing the wrong way for working out from Lime Street due to the Edge Hill turntable being out of use for maintenance. *John Corkill*

Right: In September 1958 'Princess Royal' Class 4-6-2 No 46203 *Princess Margaret Rose* is the correct way round, and not long out of Crewe Works after a heavy general repair. It has 'The Merseyside Express' headboard in place ready for a run to London Euston. The engine had just been transferred to Edge Hill from Crewe North during the week ended 20 September, and moved to Camden in August 1960. Its last allocation was Carlisle Kingmoor, where withdrawal came during the week ended 20 October 1962, but happily the 'Pacific' was saved for preservation. *John Corkill*

Left: 'Princess Royal' Class 4-6-2 No 46206 *Princess Marie Louise* was at Edge Hill on Monday 28 August 1961 when allocated to Crewe North. Entering service at Crewe North on 10 August 1935, it had two spells at Edge Hill, from 2 December 1939 to 5 April 1940 and from 25 September to 22 October 1954. It was withdrawn from Camden shed during the week ended 3 November 1962. *John Corkill*

46229

Above: The second of the original pair of 'Patriot' Class 4-6-0s, No 45501 *St Dunstans*, poses at Edge Hill on Tuesday 26 April 1960, just after transfer to Warrington Dallam shed from Mold Junction. From Warrington the engine moved to Carlisle Upperby during the week ended 10 September 1960, and was withdrawn on 26 August 1961. It was rebuilt from LNWR 'Claughton' Class 4-6-0 No 1191 at Derby Works in November 1930. *John Corkill*

Left: 'Princess Coronation' 'Pacific', No 46229 *Duchess of Hamilton*, is on standby duty at Edge Hill shed on Wednesday 12 June 1963. When transferred from Camden during the week ended 11 March 1961, the locomotive became part of the Edge Hill allocation, and remained until withdrawal during the week ended 15 February 1964. Saved for preservation, the 'Duchess' has put in many outstanding runs over the years. *John Corkill*

Above: Outside the 'new' shed at Edge Hill on Wednesday 2 June 1965 is Fairburn 4MT 2-6-4T No 42156, allocated to Birkenhead and looking to be in need of a clean. The last 2-6-4T on allocation at Edge Hill was sister engine No 42155, which was transferred away to Gorton, Manchester, during the week ended 19 January 1963, having come to Edge Hill from Bletchley in June 1954. However, a lone Stanier 2-6-4T, No 42663, was added to Edge Hill's allocation during the week ended 8 January 1966, having come from Carnforth, but after a short stay it returned during the week ended 5 February. *John Corkill*

Above: Edge Hill shed had an ex-Lancashire & Yorkshire Railway Aspinall 2F 0-6-0ST on allocation for many years, and this 1959 view shows No 51445, which had just returned to service after being stopped for firebox repairs. The engine had been on allocation since before nationalisation, but withdrawal came during the week ended 18 June 1960. *John Corkill*

Above: Ex-LMS 3F 0-6-0T No 47487 stands alongside Edge Hill shed on Tuesday 9 March 1965 with the AWS (Automatic Warning System) instruction coach, which was being used on a daily basis with a variety of locomotives. No 47487 had transferred to Edge Hill from Devons Road shed in East London during the week ended 30 December 1950, and was still at the depot when withdrawal came during the week ended 21 August 1965. *John Corkill*

Right: The replacement for No 51445 was No 51441 which arrived from Sutton Oak during the week ended 2 July 1960, and is seen here on Edge Hill shed on Monday 5 December. Withdrawal came during the week ended 18 March 1961. *John Corkill*

Above: Seen earlier, and now photographed outside the 'new' shed ready to work part of the RCTS 'Lancastrian No 2' rail tour on Saturday 20 April 1968, is Stanier 5MT 4-6-0 No 45156 *Ayrshire Yeomanry*. Looking superb and ready for the journey to come, one of the shed staff, Bob Kneale, stands in front. *John Corkill*

Above right: The shed staff were the behind-the-scenes team that ensured the efficient running of the locomotives under their care, achieving a high standard of maintenance as well as servicing engines at the depot, which was a vital part of the job. The following photographs are a tribute to the skilled shed workers and footplate crews who day in, day out made sure that Edge Hill locomotives were fit for their duties and driven and fired with enthusiasm and dedication.

The examining fitter was always a man of many years' experience, and here, armed with his long-handled hammer, he checks the top slidebar bolts on a Stanier 5MT 4-6-0 in 1958. Edge Hill usually had four examiners on its maintenance staff; all rostered main-line passenger and freight locomotives were examined on a daily basis, while trip and shunting engines were examined once a week, usually at the weekends. This highly responsible job earned the examiner 2s 6d a day above the normal fitter's rate of pay. *John Corkill*

Far left: A group of Edge Hill shed staff pose alongside Edge Hill-allocated rebuilt 'Patriot' Class 4-6-0 No 45525 *Colwyn Bay* in 1958. On the left is fitter Fred Johnson, who would be heard reciting poetry while going about his duties, including 'Into the valley of death rode the six hundred' as he disappeared into a smokebox with a duck lamp (an oil-filled lamp and wick with a naked flame, which emitted plenty of smoke). Second and third from the left are two of the shed shunt footplate staff; and behind is fitter's mate Fred Meridith. Wearing a smock and tie is leading fitter Eddy Tootle, who was always eating fruit; next is one of the six steam-raisers, and on the far right is fitter Reggie Pitchford, known as 'the gambling vicar', as he was a lay preacher at Edge Hill church and could be relied upon to give a good betting tip for any horse-racing event. *John Corkill*

Left: Posing alongside 'Princess Royal' Class 4-6-2 No 46208 *Princess Helena Victoria* in 1961 is fitter Fred Ince. He was known to all the apprentices as 'Daddy' Ince, because when they worked with him he always looked after their welfare and safety. He also ran the shed 'shop', which had large double-doored tool cupboards and was also the place to procure a steady supply of tea, sugar and condensed milk for those essential cups of tea. *John Corkill*

Above: Fitter Maurice Dickenson and his mate, ably assisted by apprentice John Corkill (on the right), use the 30-ton Ransome & Rapier steam crane to lift the front of Widnes-allocated Stanier 8F 2-8-0 No 48697, allowing access to change the engine's pony wheels. When the shed's wheel-drop was out of action, the removal of wheels had to be transferred to outside the 'new' shed, as is the case here in November 1958.

This group photo of some of Edge Hill's fitters, fitters' mates, drivers, firemen and labourers is posed in front of 'Black Five' No 45156 at the end of April 1968, with only a few days left before Edge Hill shed closed. The future for these stalwarts of the steam era was either transfer to other depots, redundancy or retirement. As for No 45156, it was transferred to Manchester Patricroft, then finally to Rose Grove, and was itself made 'redundant' by withdrawal during the week ended 10 August 1968. *John Corkill*

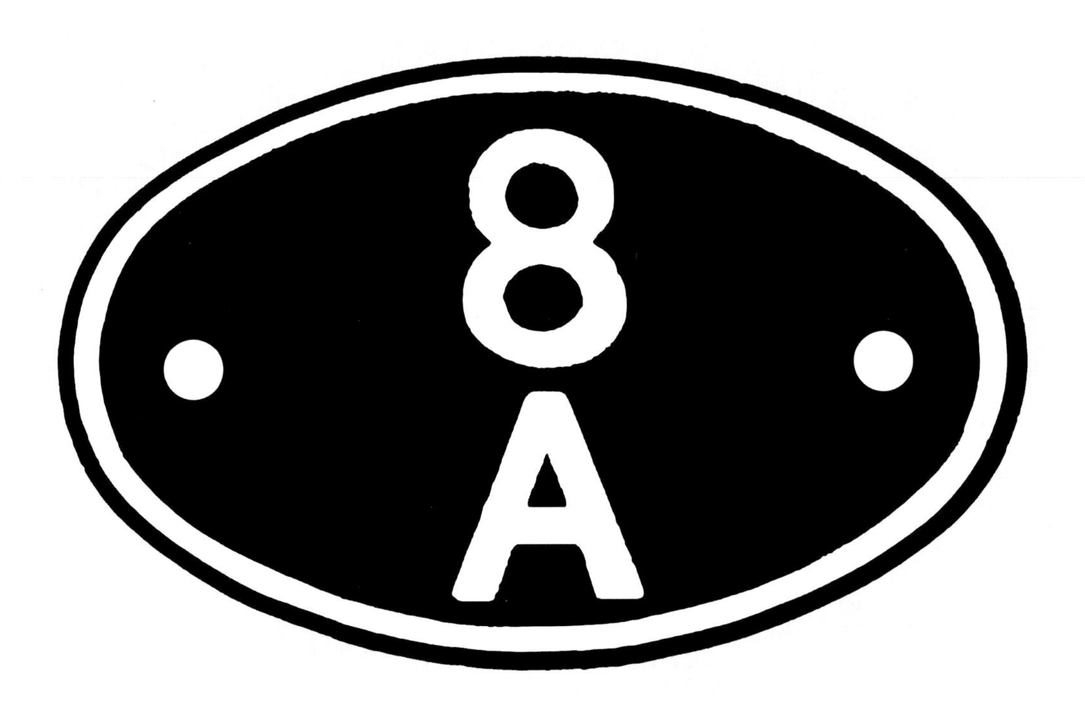

45156

Index of locations and locomotive classes

Locations

Locomotive classes

BR

GWR

LMS

LNER

SR